WEST BROMWICH
REVISITED

OLD PARISH CHURCH
WEST BROMWICH

The Smith family in 1934 at Spon Cottage which was built in 1861. Back row, left to right: Lilian, Ernie, Ivy. Middl row: Ada (mother), Beatrice, Elsie, Ernest (father – formerly a brass-caster then a bookmaker), Margaret (on mother lap), David. Front row: Eileen and Betty (twins). Two other daughters aged four and eighteen had already died (Mrs M. Hemming)

BRITAIN IN OLD PHOTOGRAPHS

WEST BROMWICH REVISITED

DAVID F. VODDEN

SUTTON PUBLISHING LIMITED

Sutton Publishing Limited
Phoenix Mill · Thrupp · Stroud
Gloucestershire · GL5 2BU

First published 1999

Half-title page photograph: All Saints' Church, 1904 (Dr C. Hollingsworth); *title page photograph*: The West Bromwich Coat of Arms was granted in 1882. The motto, *Labor Omnia Vincit*, means 'Work conquers all'. The crest is a stag and ostrich feathers from the arms of the Earls of Dartmouth. The shield bears a stag's head representing the Earls of Dartmouth, the mullets (stars) and fleurs-de-lys around the border represent Sandwell Hall, ancestral home of the Dartmouths. Gold millrinds (clamps found at the centres of mill wheels) symbolise metal-based industries. This example is from the gates of the Memorial Gardens off the High Street.

British Library Cataloguing in Publication Data
A catalogue record for this book is available from the British Library.

ISBN 0-7509-1897-7

Typeset in 10/11 Bembo.
Typesetting and origination by
Sutton Publishing Limited.
Printed in Great Britain by
Ebenezer Baylis, Worcester.

THE BLACK COUNTRY SOCIETY

This voluntary society, affiliated to the Civic Trust, was founded in 1967 as a reaction to the trend of the late 1950s and early 1960s to amalgamate everything into large units and in the Midlands to sweep away the area's industrial heritage in the process.

The general aim of the Society is to create interest in the past, present and future of the Black Country, and early on it campaigned for the establishment of an industrial museum. In 1975 the Black Country Museum was started by Dudley Borough Council on 26 acres of totally derelict land adjoining the grounds of Dudley Castle. This has developed into an award-winning museum which attracts over 250,000 visitors annually.

At the Black Country Museum there is a boat dock fully equipped to restore narrow boats of wood and iron and different boats can be seen on the dock throughout the year. From behind the Bottle and Glass Inn visitors can travel on a canal boat into Dudley Canal Tunnel, a memorable journey to see spectacular limestone caverns and the fascinating Castle Mill Basin.

There are over two thousand members of the Black Country Society and all receive the quarterly magazine *The Blackcountryman*, of which over 119 issues have been published since its founding in 1967. In the whole collection there are some 1,700 authoritative articles on all aspects of the Black Country by historians, teachers, researchers, students, subject experts and ordinary folk with an extraordinary story to tell. The whole constitutes a unique resource about the area and is a mine of information for students and researchers who frequently refer to it. Many schools and libraries are subscribers. Three thousand copies of the magazine are printed each quarter. It is non-commercial, and contributors do not receive payment for their articles.

PO Box 71 · Kingswinford · West Midlands DY6 9YN

CONTENTS

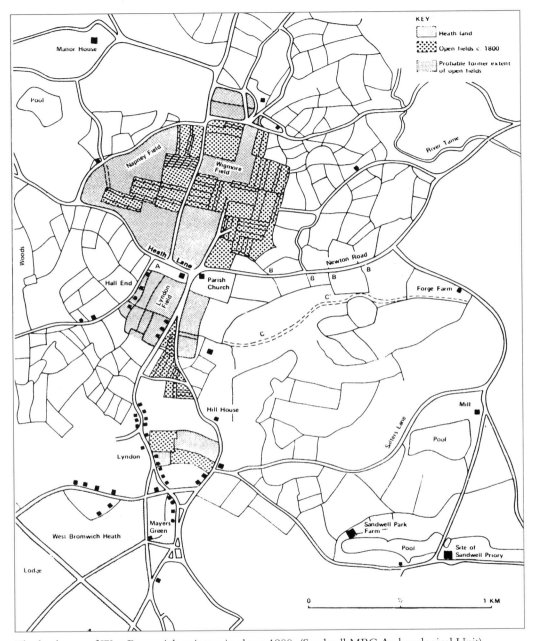

The landscape of West Bromwich as it was in about 1800. (Sandwell MBC Archaeological Unit)

INTRODUCTION

West Bromwich, so called to distinguish it from Castle Bromwich or Little Bromwich, has a very long history, as one can judge from the 'Bromwich' part of its name. It derives from 'Bromwic' of the Anglo-Saxon period and the word means 'a village where broom grows'.

West Bromwich was listed in the Domesday Book of 1086, when there were about sixty inhabitants. The earliest parts of All Saints' Church are thought to be Norman. It was at the centre of the medieval village, surrounded by the typical great open fields such as Wigmore Field, Napney Field and Lyndon Field – these are now covered by modern housing, a cemetery and the Sandwell District Hospital.

The siting of West Bromwich's modern town centre is the result of industrialisation, which began in small ways as early as the twelfth and thirteenth centuries. Some of the oldest mills are identifiable from the sixteenth century, long before the Industrial Revolution of the eighteenth; however, much of the town's growth took place during the nineteenth century and brought with it a population explosion and consequent housing development.

By 1380, soon after the Black Death, there were only about 160 inhabitants. Increased prosperity towards the end of the Middle Ages meant that by 1563 there were approximately 834 inhabitants. At the time of the Civil War the number had risen to about 1,383. The first national census in 1801 indicated 5,687 and this had grown by the time of the Great Exhibition in 1851 to 34,600. Considerable expansion took place by the end of the nineteenth century so that in 1901 the figure was 65,100. Despite the ravages of the First World War the figure was 73,800 in 1921. By the outbreak of the Second World War there were 83,150 and by 1951 – the year of the Festival of Britain – the total was 88,000. Following the enlargement of the boundaries in 1966, the population in 1969 was 172,000. Currently, it stands at around 290,000 but this also reflects the expansion of the Borough in 1974.

Nowadays, West Bromwich is at the heart of Sandwell Metropolitan Borough along with the five other formerly separate towns of Oldbury, Rowley Regis, Smethwick, Tipton and Wednesbury. The name Sandwell comes from the site of the twelfth-century Benedictine Priory which had a holy *sanct* (well).

A new tablet on the north wall of All Saints' Church relates some details of the influence of Sandwell Priory. Following the Suppression, the site of the Priory eventually came into the possession of the Whorwood family whose effigies are in the church. The family of the future Earls of Dartmouth acquired it in 1701 and built their own Sandwell Hall in 1705, eventually demolished in the 1920s. To the Earls of Dartmouth, West Bromwich owed a great deal; they introduced coal-mining to the area, made available 56 acres for Dartmouth Park and, in this century, the Earl gave the town Forge Mill Farm.

Other principal benefactors included Reuben Farley JP, who not only persuaded the Earl to provide land for Dartmouth Park, but also, for his part, gave the sixteenth-century Oak House to the town as a museum, and Farley Park. He is commemorated by the 67 ft clock tower at Carter's Green.

Not only was West Bromwich the home of many manufacturers who were to become household names such as Izons, Salter's, Jensen, Bean, Tangye and Kenrick and Jefferson, the town and its firms introduced many inventions: Tangye's hydraulic jacks were used to launch ships such as Brunel's *Great Eastern*; Chance's glass glazed the Crystal Palace at the Great Exhibition in 1851; Salter's have not only produced a weighing machine capable of handling 200 tons, but also pioneered the first all-British typewriter in 1895.

Reflecting its economic prosperity, the High Street stretched for a mile down to Carter's Green at the west end. It used to be known as the 'Golden Mile' with a good mix of fine public buildings and quality retailers. The development of such new shopping malls as the Sandwell Centre has tended to concentrate attention on the middle of the High Street. Nevertheless, some businesses such as the West Bromwich Building Society have built substantial and fine new office buildings at 374 High Street.

To many, West Bromwich is exemplified by the West Bromwich Albion Football Club which had its beginnings in the nineteenth century as 'The Strollers', a Salter's Works team.

There were many successful individuals who owed their start in life to West Bromwich: Sir Richard Shelton was Solicitor General from 1625 to 1634 as was Lord Peter Archer in more recent times. William Legge's family bought Sandwell Hall and became Earls of Dartmouth. The fifth son of the fourth Earl, Augustus Legge, became Bishop of Lichfield in 1891. Francis Asbury, born in 1745, became the first Methodist Bishop in America and his family home still survives. In more recent times, J.J. Shaw became internationally respected for his work on earthquakes and developed a type of seismograph which continues to be in use throughout the world.

Lord Raymond P. Brookes of West Bromwich is a good example of 'local boy makes good'. Having left school early, he persisted through evening classes and correspondence courses as well as serving an apprenticeship with Charles Bunn Ltd to become Chairman and Managing Director of a number of firms, until he became Chairman of GKN and is currently their Life President as well as being created a peer.

Alan Pitt had a long career in the building industry which was matched by considerable public service. He worked hard for the WEA (Workers Educational Association) and, in 1968, was proud to receive his Social Science degree from Birmingham University. As a Justice of the Peace he worked hard on the West Midlands Probation Committee and the Central Probation Committee as Deputy Chairman and Treasurer, as well as becoming Chairman of the West Bromwich Bench.

In the world of entertainment, leading actresses from the area include Madeleine Carroll of the 1930s and more recently Julie Walters, while Jack Judge was the author of the famous song 'It's a long way to Tipperary'.

In the world of politics, television and political commentary, Brian Walden stands out. He attended West Bromwich Grammar School, but has referred to his childhood in the Stone Cross area as 'the best of times, the best of places'. West Bromwich also has a soft spot for Betty Boothroyd MP who entered Parliament as MP for West Bromwich in 1973 and, while having become Speaker of the House of Commons, still works hard as a constituency MP.

West Bromwich has had a long history, mostly concerned with the manufacturing industry, and has produced many very able people who have shown great concern for the welfare of their community.

CHAPTER ONE

STREET SCENES

An aerial view of the High Street west end, showing a large section of what used to be nicknamed the 'Golden Mile', November 1997. (D. Wilkins, First House Photography)

An aerial view of the High Street from the south-east, November 1997. (D. Wilkins, First House Photography)

An aerial view of the High Street and bus station, November 1997. (D. Wilkins, First House Photography)

The High Street, showing the Farley Fountain which was removed to Dartmouth Park in 1911. See page 107 (Dr C. Hollingsworth)

The High Street. (Dr C. Hollingsworth)

The High Street. (J.S. Webb)

Dartmouth Square showing the Spon Lane junction, *c.* 1911. The remains of the Paradise Street horse-drawn tram track are just visible. The Farley Fountain had been removed in 1911 and replaced by the clock. See page 107. (J.S. Webb)

High Street, 1910. The building with mock battlements, built as a house, served as a pharmacy – the Provident Medical Dispensary from 1866. (Dr C. Hollingsworth)

The Town Hall, 1905. (Dr C. Hollingsworth)

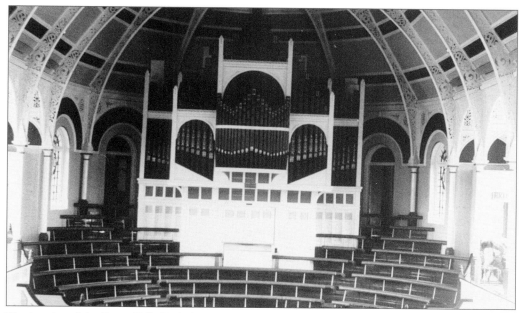

The interior of the Town Hall, 1979. (BCS/BCM)

Farley Clock Tower, nicknamed 'the pepperpot', but described as 'gothic/renaissance'. This was erected at Carter's Green in honour of Alderman Reuben Farley in 1897, two years before his death. (Dr C. Hollingsworth)

Farley Clock Tower, 1904.
(Dr C. Hollingsworth)

Farley Clock Tower, 1998. The Wesleyan chapel,
built between 1875 and 1876 and visible in the
previous picture, has now been demolished.

Carter's Green Medical Centre and shops, 384 High Street, was the practice from which the doctor's letter came (see page 92).

West Bromwich Building Society's head office. The Society, founded in 1849, was situated at 402 Lower High Street from 1854, and acquired premises at 298 High Street in 1868, built 301 High Street in 1879 and another site at 321 High Street in 1927. The present building was opened in October 1978.

The Old Post Office dates from 1918 and is
now a restaurant. It replaced the earlier
premises such as that established in 1828 in
Dartmouth Street.

Kenrick & Jefferson's former works in the High Street. The first phase, on the far left of the picture, was
completed in 1883 and is a grade II listed building. The newer wing (right) was completed in 1928.
'K & J' have recently moved out of the High Street and new uses are to be found for the buildings.

The old Police Station at Stone Cross opposite All Saints' Church, 1969. There used to be accommodation for single policemen in this building and stabling at the rear for police horses. Stabling is currently provided at the new station in New Street. (BCS/BCM)

The High Street looking east from the ring road and Dartmouth Square, 1998.

Beeches Road, 1911. This was laid out by G.B. Nicholls in the 1860s in a previously wooded area adjacent to Sandwell Park, and established itself as a well-to-do suburb in the 1880s. In the picture the trees appear to have been recently planted. (Dr C. Hollingsworth)

The Avenue, Grove Crescent, 1912. This was a similar suburban development on the south side of Birmingham Road. Grove House itself used to stand in a 4-acre plot. (Dr C. Hollingsworth)

An early view of Holloway Bank, showing a horse and carriage. This photograph looks in the direction of Wednesbury, down what was once known as Finchpath Hill. Its name was changed after the gradient was reduced in the seventeenth century to provide for the carriage of heavy loads of coal. (J.S. Webb)

A selection of parked vehicles belonging to William Arnold & Sons, plumbers' merchants. (A.H. Price)

Demolition of Spencers' Bakery, at the corner of Sandwell Road, 1969. (BCS/BCM)

The Grange Bakery used to stand at the corner of Grange Road and Dartmouth Street opposite the Loving Lamb, and is seen here in about 1905. The bakery belonged to Edwin Standing. Holding the horse is his son Harry, and grandson Fred is on the cart. The shop is now a small corner shop. (B. Wilkes)

The main entrance to Dartmouth Park with the Lodge, 1905. The 56-acre park was given to the town by the Earl of Dartmouth in 1877. (Dr C. Hollingsworth)

Cemetery gates, Heath Lane. The cemetery was established in 1859. (Dr C. Hollingsworth)

The Old Stone Cross Inn at Stone Cross. The cross, from which it took its name, stood on a red sandstone base. Thomas Sheldon, who owned the adjoining blacksmith's shop, obtained a licence for the house in about 1805. The Martin family were licensees from 1872. (BCS/BCM)

The Old Stone Cross Inn early in the twentieth century, by which time the stone cross had been replaced with an iron one with a gas street lamp on top. Frank Fox was landlord when this picture was taken. This building was demolished in 1928 and the present pub was built in 1932. (BCS/BCM)

The Turks Head Inn, at the corner of Sams Lane and Bromford Lane in the Lyng area of the town, *c.* 1912. At this time Henry Stevens was licensee. (BCS/BCM)

The Turks Head bar, *c.* 1912. The barmaids are Eliza Stevens and her daughter Nelly Stevens, later Doorbar, who died in 1968 aged seventy-three. (R. Holden)

The Yew Tree Inn, Albion Road. The inn was closed one week later, on 30 June 1963. The new Yew Tree has been built nearby. (A.H. Price)

The Goose and Granite pub on the corner of the High Street and New Street, 1998. This was formerly known as the Sandwell Hotel.

A view of Spon Lane in the 1920s showing the tramlines and on the right, just behind the low wall, stood Spon Cottage (see page 2). (Mrs M. Hemming)

Sunnyside, 77a Birmingham Road, was formerly the home of J.J. Shaw, known as 'the earthquake man', for his work in seismology. It is seen here in 1994. (Dr J. Lester)

Oldbury town square, 1900. The town's Grammar School was founded in 1904. The motto of the Urban District Council read 'Let its ancient glory flourish', and by 1935 Oldbury had developed to the point where it became a Borough and elected K.H. Wilson as its first mayor. (Mrs F. Allen)

Oldbury town square with its cenotaph, spring 1952. In 1966 Oldbury lost its independence when it became part of Warley. In 1974 it became part of Sandwell. (Mrs F. Allen)

CHAPTER TWO

CHURCHES

All Saints' Church and cottages, c. 1907. The cottages have long since been demolished.
(I. Bott)

Christ Church was built in 1826 and designed by Francis Goodwin. It stood just off the High Street, and is seen here in 1904. Following a serious fire on 23 October 1979 it was demolished. (Dr C. Hollingsworth)

The site of the former Christ Church is now occupied by the JobCentre.

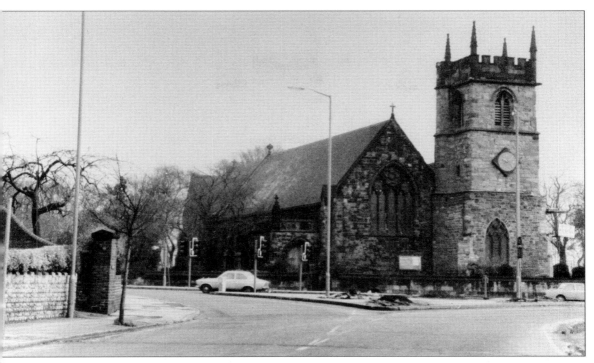

A view of All Saints' Church in 1975 for a new illustrated guide. (A.H. Price)

All Saints' Church interior, 1914. Since then, the pulpit has been moved away from the north wall and the lighting modernised. (Dr C. Hollingsworth)

This Norman pillar and floor tiles have been set in the wall of the former ringing chamber of All Saints' Church, now the church office. They are all that remain of the old church, which was replaced in 1872.

All Saints' Church font standing at the back of the church, 1975. It has since been moved to the front. (A.H. Price)

The oak choir stalls are one of the main features of All Saints' Church and date from 1898. The bench ends are carved to represent the Services and Sacraments. This carving represents 'Confirmation'. (A.H. Price)

All Saints' Church choir stall representing 'Blessing'. (A.H. Price)

All Saints' Church choir stall representing 'Marriage'. (A.H. Price)

All Saints' Church choir stall representing 'Visiting the sick'. (A.H. Price)

All Saints' Church Whorwood memorial lying under the arcading between the chancel and the Lady Chapel in 1975. They have since been propped up against the south wall. (A.H. Price)

Memorial to Captain James Eaton RN opposite the south door of All Saints' Church. He was present at the Battle of Trafalgar on 21 October 1805 and served on the *Temeraire*. As a Signal Midshipman he had the honour of repeating Nelson's famous signal prior to the battle. He died in 1857 at Hill House which was in Dagger Lane.

The Baptist Church gallery, early 1970s. The High Street site is now occupied by the West Bromwich Building Society (see page 17). (BCS/BCM)

The Wesley monument has recently been erected in the High Street to commemorate the strong local links with John Wesley.

Wesleyan Church, High Street, 1998. This stands on the site of an earlier church. On 11 December 1971 the Mayor, Councillor Bill Manifold, relaid the foundation stone of 1904 which was turned around with a new inscription on it.

A plaque depicting John Wesley on the new Wesleyan Church in the High Street.

St Michael's Roman Catholic Church from across the ring road, November 1998. This church dates from 1877 and was designed by Dunn and Hansom. The spire was added in 1911.

A steam tram outside St Michael's Roman Catholic Church, 1890s. (J.S. Webb)

CHAPTER THREE

TRANSPORT

A specially posed group comprising Crowther horse car, South Staffordshire electric tram and steam tram at Dartmouth Square, December 1902. (J.S. Webb)

Original track-laying at Carter's Green, 1880s. (J.S. Webb)

South Staffordshire Trams steam locomotive No. 12 near Christ Church, 1890s. Note the track relaying taking place. (J.S. Webb)

South Staffordshire Trams' steam tram, High Street, with the Town Hall in the background, *c.* 1900. (J.S. Webb)

Steam tram No. 7 at Handsworth Depot. (J.S. Webb)

Steam tram near Bagnall Street on Birmingham Road. Engine no. 3 is drawing a 1–12 class car. (J.S. Webb)

Handsworth boundary showing the blocking of tramway services by a Handsworth Council steamroller, owing to a through-running controversy. The South Staffordshire Tramways had signed an agreement with West Bromwich on 8 September 1903 for electric tram operating. Without completing a lease with Handsworth (where the depot stood), the company connected up the trolley wires temporarily with those of West Bromwich in the early morning of 10 September. Handsworth Highways Department took immediate action and prevented any further company tram invasions for that day. The lease was eventually completed and the service began on 1 October 1904. The Handsworth Tram Depot shed has now been set up at the Black Country Museum.

10–27 class Brush bogie cars, Carter's Green, on opening day. The official party is preparing for the inaugural run, 1902. (J.S. Webb)

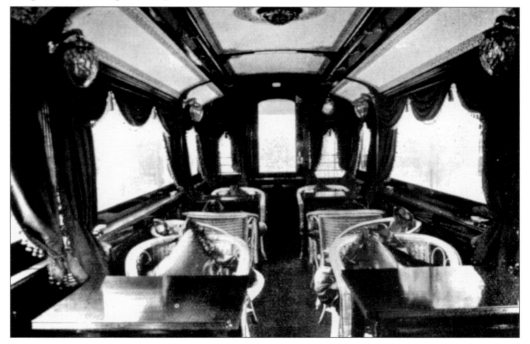

South Staffordshire Tramways Directors' saloon interior as first fitted. These were used in the early years for opening routes as well as for Directors' inspections. This body was eventually used as a clothes store at Hartshill Depot. (J.S. Webb)

Tram car no. 22 on the Wednesbury route at Carter's Green. (J.S. Webb)

Farley Clock Tower with an open-top tram heading for Wednesbury. (J.S. Webb)

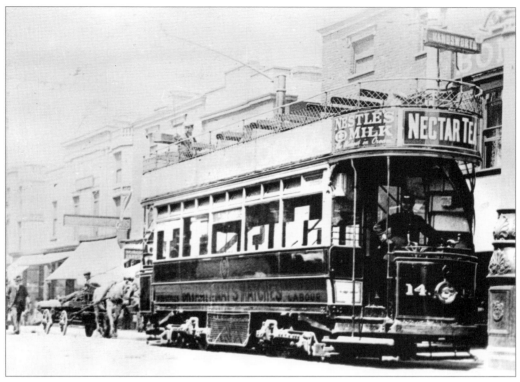

Tram car no. 14 at Dartmouth Square, just before the First World War. (J.S. Webb)

Tram car at the corner of High Street and St Michael's Street looking towards Carter's Green. This card was posted in 1923. (J.S. Webb)

Tram car no. 5 at Dartmouth Square on the Great Bridge service, *c.* 1905. (J.S. Webb)

'Lye'-type tram waiting for passengers in Dartmouth Square, 1929. (BCS/BCM)

A Churchill charabanc, 1912. (J. Boulton)

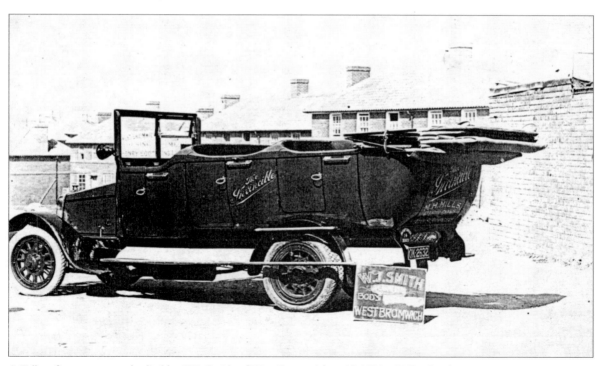

A Talbot fourteen-seater bodied by W.J. Smith of West Bromwich, mid-1920s. (J. Boulton)

J. Robinson motor bus outing, *c.* 1920. (BCS/BCM)

Braithwaite charabancs, 6 July 1929. (K. Hodgkins/H. Alsopp)

Leyland coach belonging to A. Walsgrove's Throstle Tours, 1935. (J. Boulton)

Jensen coach built on a JNSN chassis, which was also popular for flat-bed trailers and pantechnicons, c. 1949. (J. Boulton)

A 1930s Dennis West Bromwich Corporation bus during the Second World War, as indicated by the headlamp masks. (J. Boulton)

West Bromwich Corporation bus EA 4181. (A.H. Price)

x-West Bromwich Corporation bus CEA 174, 1975. (A.H. Price)

. bus rally in Dartmouth Park, 1975. (BCS/BCM)

A Guy van belonging to Siddons Ltd, 1920. Siddons manufactured cast-iron holloware until it went out of fashion in favour of aluminium. (J. Boulton)

AEC lorry belonging to T. Wheatley & Son of West Bromwich, *c.* 1920. (J. Boulton)

Steel sheet lorry, *c.* 1934. (J. Boulton)

This was the third lightweight, single axle, 4 ton lorry to be commissioned from Jensen by Reynolds Tube. It went into service in 1940. (J. Boulton)

YS — A STRIKING RESULT

Chassisless Construction Carried out by Jensen Motors
Vehicles Make the Design Student Think

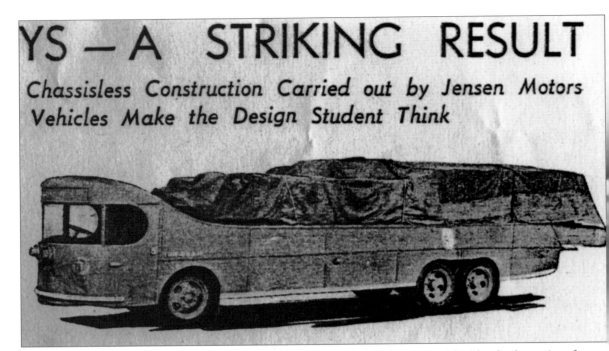

This chassisless lorry was designed by Jensen to transport up to 30 ft lengths of material with a load capacity of up to 5 tons. It was powered by a Ford four-cylinder engine and entered service in 1939. (J. Boulton)

A 3.5-litre Jensen Tourer, 1939. The first Jensen Special was built in 1928 and in 1934 the company adopted the name Jensen Motors Ltd. The following year the first 3.5-litre model was announced. Regrettably, the company finally ceased trading in 1993 – but rights to the Jensen name were acquired in 1992 by Creative Group Ltd, who unveiled the all-new S-V8 roadster at the British International Motor Show in 1998. The company is now based in Redditch. (J. Boulton)

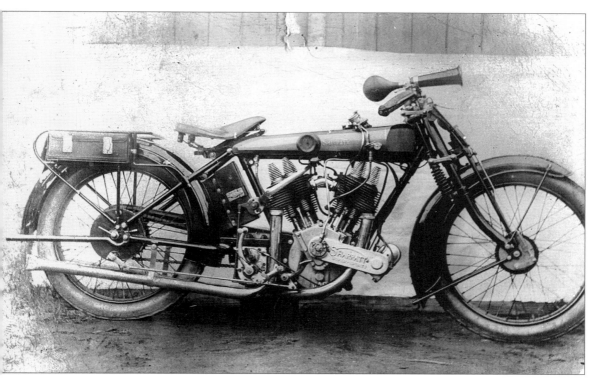

A 1923 V twin Super Sports Sharratt motorcycle manufactured at Carter's Green.(J. Boulton)

The West Bromwich Corporation steamroller, *c.* 1900. (K. Hodgkins)

Steam at Swan Village in the 1960s. This is GWR 5033 'Broughton Castle'. (BCS/BCM)

Engine no. 6922 'Burton Hall', again at Swan Village. (BCS/BCM)

CHAPTER FOUR

SCHOOLS

Hall Green Infants School was opened with the Junior School in 1940 and is an excellent example of the high quality school buildings which were constructed at that time. (M. Allen)

The former West Bromwich Grammar School, founded as the West Bromwich Institute in 1886, has been a Department of the Technical College since 1964. The West Bromwich Institute still meets in the Lecture Room. A new grammar school was built at Marsh Lane in 1964 to the designs of Richard Shepherd Robson & Partners. With reorganisation it became a comprehensive school and was renamed Menzies High School in honour of the first Grammar School headmaster, A.J. Menzies, who retired in 1932.

West Bromwich Grammar School sixth form, c. 1935. Back row, left to right: A. Faulkner, -?-, Arnold Blackwell, -?-, Gilbert Phillips, Gerald Lush, Guy Ellison, Stanley Prince. Front row: -?-, Dorothy Stamp, -?-, Mr Cockroft, -?-, -?-, -?-, Molly Round. (G.R. Phillips)

The old West Bromwich Grammar School after a severe fire on 9 April 1976. For some years the building had been part of the Technical College and the top floor housed the engineering department. (J.S. Hunt)

The old Grammar School from above, after the fire, 1976. The Borough Council decided eventually not to rebuild the top floor, but to reduce the height of the building and replace the roof. In the meantime, the engineering classes were moved to another site belonging to the college at Wednesbury. (J.S. Hunt)

The former Ryland Art College, which had been separated from the Institute before it became the Grammar School or part of the Technical College. It has a very finely decorated brick façade and dates from 1906.

Children at Lyng School, Horton Street, 1922. (BCS/BCM)

Yew Tree Infant pupils with their teacher Mrs Maureen Wilkes, 1958. (M. Wilkes)

Yew Tree Infants on the playing field with Mrs Wilkes, 1958. (M. Wilkes)

Black Lake Infants' nativity play, 1961. (M. Wilkes)

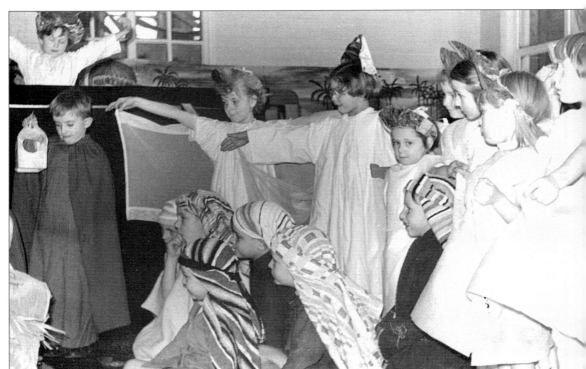

lack Lake Infants School, top class girls, 1962. (M. Wilkes)

lack Lake Infants School, top class boys, 1962. (M. Wilkes)

West Bromwich schools camp in the Forest of Dean, 1960. (M. Wilkes)

West Bromwich schools camp, Yew Tree School pupils. (M. Wilkes)

Hall Green Infants with some of the fruit and bread at their harvest festival, 1968. After the service the food was given to the WRVS for distribution to the elderly as part of their 'meals on wheels' service – some of the children accompanied them. (E. Cartwright)

Hall Green Nursery nativity play, c. 1970. The nativity scene background became a permanent feature and was made of marquetry by first year pupils of Menzies High School. Half the Hall Green juniors transferred to Menzies High School at the age of eleven each year. (M. Allen)

Hall Green top infants, *c.* 1970. This class remained together throughout their time in primary school. (M. Allen)

Hall Green staff, *c.* 1970. Back row, left to right: Jennifer Stocking, Christine Kelsey, -?-, -?-, -?-, Ann Firkins. Front row: Jennifer Austin, Brenda Wiseman, Elsie Cartwright (Deputy Head), Margaret Allen (Head), Joan Marshall, Pauline Dawson, Doreen Evans (Secretary). (M. Allen)

Hall Green pupils presenting a table to Bromford House home for the elderly on 20 July 1977. Class teacher Miss Dent's aunt, Miss Isa Spears of Dollar, Clackmannanshire, provided the money for the table. (M. Allen)

Hall Green Infants presenting a picture to the Matron, Mrs Bennett, at Bromford House home for the elderly. (E. Cartwright)

Mrs Heywood, the Deputy Head's retirement, July 1973. Here are some of Class 1He in Hall Green School garden. Left to right: Paul Tyler, Yvonne Pearce, Denise Edwards, Andrew Leadbeater, Sally Morris, Neil Whatnall, Gary Goddard (hidden), Wendy James, Stephanie Price, Karen Bull. (M. Allen)

Mrs Edna Cadman, nursery teacher at Hall Green Infants' School, is presented with a Teasmade by Headmistress, Mrs Margaret Allen, on her retirement, Easter 1979. Staff looking on are, left to right, Jean Mansell, -?-, Elsie Cartwright (Deputy Head), Jennifer Stocking, Ann Firkins, Doreen Evans (Secretary) Margaret Taylor, Maggie Brookes, Chris Kelsey, Brenda Wiseman. (E. Cartwright)

Headmistress Mrs Margaret Allen retires from Hall Green Infants' School, July 1979. (E. Cartwright)

Hamstead Junior School staff, Great Barr, 1976. Back row, left to right: Bessie Mitchell, Madelain ?, Hilda Sells, Lynsey Worwick, Kath Colley, Margaret Franks, Pat ?, Valerie Smith, Janet Withers, Pat ?, -?-. Front row: Linsey ?, Brian Wilkes, Jean Vale, Jack Shipley, Mel Earnshaw, Jill Banister, Margaret ?, Ann Lewis. (B. Wilkes)

Hamstead Junior School, 1992. Front to back: ten-year-olds Jane Shuttleworth, Jane Thackwood, Jillian Hughes, Samantha Gardner and Vicky Saxton. (Sandwell MBC Education Department)

Victorian Day at St Martin's Church of England Primary School, 1992. Left to right: Amy Hawkes (ten), Helen Duffield (eight), Paul Smith (eight), Hayley Whitehouse (seven), Ashley Townsend (nine) and Stephen Foster (ten) (standing behind). (Sandwell MBC Education Department)

The mayor, Councillor Sullivan, and Jeffrey Archer open the school library, 13 November 1992. It is now regarded as one of the finest primary school libraries in the country. The mayoress Mrs Kerton's twin children were pupils at the school. (Sandwell MBC Education Department)

Councillor Tarsem King, Education Committee Chairman, opens Education Week in Queen's Square to commemorate the establishment of schools in West Bromwich for over a hundred years, 1992. (Sandwell MBC Education Department)

Alan Pitt with other tutors and students at Winterbourne, University of Birmingham Extra-mural Department, June 1975. The students were from Birfield Extrusions, GKN, Hamstead, Birmingham, and they were attending a 'Work and Wealth' WEA course. Alan Pitt stands far left and fourth from left is Philip Elliott. (P.J. Elliott)

Alan Pitt, after receiving his B.Soc.Sci. degree at the Congregation at the University of Birmingham, July 1968. He is seen here with sons David and Adrian and wife, Irene. Alan Pitt was also keen on local history. He is regarded as an expert on Bustleholme Mill (see pages 82–5). (P.J. Elliott)

CHAPTER FIVE

WORK

Ironworkers at Samuel Downing & Sons, Richmond Ironworks, Great Bridge, 1913. The firm were in business from 1880. The number of men suggests that this is the complete mill team, including furnacemen, shearers and labourers. The older man at the extreme right of the front row is probably the roller (or foreman) in charge of the team. The exact meaning of the term 'Big Mill' cannot be established, but it was probably a 10- or 12-in mill. Three of the people pictured are definitely not part of the mill team – the two young men (extreme right and left of the back row) are office staff, and the little girl (front row, extreme left). No females, adults or children, were ever employed at the mill. It is most likely that she had brought breakfast or dinner for one or more of the men; this was a common practice. The size of her basket suggests several meals.(BCS/BCM)

Furnace bricklayers at Samuel Downing & Sons, 1913. Furnace brickies often had to work in confined spaces in furnaces, with wet refractory cement all around, hence the state of the men's clothes. (BCS/BCM)

A furnaceman (left) and his two underhands, standing in front of a reheating furnace, 1913. On the right (in the foreground) there is a pile of horseshoes which would be piled, heated, shingled to blooms and re-rolled into finished products. (BCS/BCM)

A puddler (right) and underhand, pig iron, Samuel Downing's, 1913. The underhand is holding the ball tongs used for pulling the puddled balls out of the furnace. (BCS/BCM)

A complete rollingmill team at Samuel Downing's, 1913. (BCS/BCM)

Sandwell Casting Co., pattern shop. (BCS/BCM)

Harry Peach core-making for the interior shape of brass bells at Sandwell Casting Co., Bank Street. (BCS/BCM)

Handbell castings await machining at the Sandwell Casting Co., 2 May 1968.(A.H. Price)

A worker machines bell castings at Sandwell Casting Co., 1955. This order was for the Admiralty, which was the company's largest customer for bells. They also manufactured bells for the Home Office for use in Borstal institutions. (BCS/BCM)

Brass casting at Sandwell Casting Co., 1974. (A.H. Price)

Brass casting at Sandwell Casting Co., July 1972. (A.H. Price)

Conex Sanbra trap shop at West Bromwich, *c.* 1968. Sanbra moved to join Conex at Great Bridge in that year. Here copper tubing is being manipulated to the required shape and size for the assembly of bath and kitchen wastefittings. (A.H. Price)

Brian Paddock threading bathroom fittings at Conex, West Bromwich, 1954. (BCS/BCM)

Conex Sanbra Polishing Shop. Here brass fittings are being polished before being chromium plated. (A.H. Price)

Sanbra machine shop at Aston, 1950. (BCS/BCM)

Casting leaving the works of Rudge, Witley & Co., *c.* 1900. (BCS/BCM)

Bustleholme Mill, 1968. (A.H. Price)

Bustleholme Mill as it was in 1968. It was demolished in 1971 to make way for the M5 motorway. Mills had been built on this site as early as 1594 and their purposes developed from a slitting-mill for slitting iron bars made at local forges to a corn-mill, operated by an undershot or low-breast wheel. It appears to have been a corn-mill in 1709 as well as having produced iron rod. It was still working as late as the 1890s. (A.H. Price)

Bustleholme Mill, 24 February 1968. (A.H. Price)

Bustleholme Mill, 24 February 1968. (A.H. Price)

Bustleholme Mill, March 1968. (A.H. Price)

Bustleholme Mill interior showing burr stones and wooden driveshaft, June 1968. (A.H. Price)

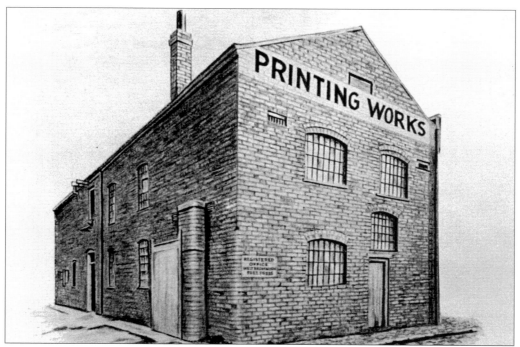

Kenrick & Jefferson's works, 1878. This drawing by A. Freeman shows the original works which was also the registered office of the Free Press. (K&J)

Manifold Printing Works, 1914. It was founded in a former Salvation Army barracks in Queen Street in 1903 and moved to a new Bromford Lane factory after five years. They were 'printers, lithographers, manufacturers' stationers and manufacturers of calendars'. Manifold were eventually taken over by Lamson Paragon but have long since closed down. (Mrs F. Allen)

Salter's scales works, George Street, *c.* 1970. Salter's are long-established manufacturers of weighing machines, springs and scales and now trade as Salter Weightronics. (BCS/BCM)

Salter standard typewriter, 1905. Salter's typewriters were manufactured at the George Street works from 1895 to 1936. After that date the typewriter division became a separate company, and later part of Smith Corona. (J. Boulton)

JOHN BULL: "It makes me tired to hear the Yankee talk Typewriters. Why, the British-made SALTER beats them all.

"You should write to my friends, The SALTER TYPEWRITER CO., of WEST BROMWICH, for particulars of their unique Rental Scheme.

"It will interest you, especially as they are the ONLY Standard Typewriter Makers in Great Britain."

Salter's typewriter advertisement on a postcard. This was the first all-British typewriter and was produced from 1895. The postcard is from the 1920s. (Dr C. Hollingsworth)

Offices of Izons, the first cast-iron holloware manufacturers in England. The company was established in 1760 in Aston, and moved to a mill in West Bromwich in the 1780s. John Izon and Thomas Whitehurst were partners from 1763. John Izon's second son, William, bought Lodge Farm in 1822 as a home. Its name is perpetuated in Lodge Road.(BCS/BCM)

Boilerhouse generators at Izons' works. (BCS/BCM)

Wigmore Farm overshadowed by council flats, 1968. It was farmed within living memory by the Thompson family and, although some buildings were demolished during the construction of the M5, the core remained in use as a riding school. (BCS/BCM)

Hill House Farm, Church Vale, 1969. The farm was basically a Tudor building and had belonged to the Grove family of Dagger Hall and later Captain Eaton RN who died there in 1857. (BCS/BCM)

Hill House farmyard. (BCS/BCM)

Forge Farm, *c.* 1910. The farm, comprising 77 acres, was sold by the Earl of Dartmouth to the Council in the 1920s, and it remained unaltered. Nearby was Forge Mill dating from the early seventeenth century. (BCS/BCM)

Hamstead Colliery, situated on the South Staffordshire coalfield, suffered a major disaster in 1908 in which twenty-five men were killed. Production ceased in March 1965 because of geological faults. (A.H. Price)

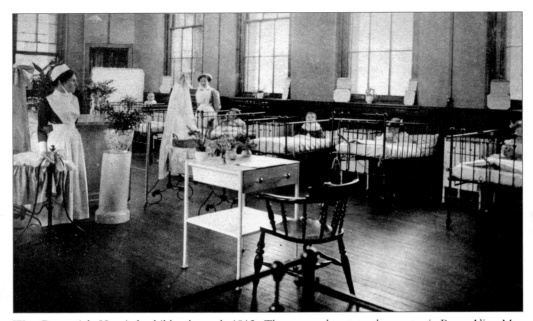

West Bromwich Hospital, children's ward, 1912. The nurse closest to the centre is Rose Alice May Osborne SRN (née Devey). (Mrs C. Walters)

AT HOME:
9-30 TO 10-30 A.M.
6 TO 7-30 P.M.
TELEPHONE TOY.

Nov 1907.

Dear Sir or Madam,

As you have hitherto been one of my patients, I take this opportunity of informing you that I have taken into partnership Dr A. C. Goodwin, late of Oxford University and the London Hospital.

Dr Goodwin is a Bachelor of Medicine, and Master of Surgery of Oxford, and a Fellow of the Royal College of Surgeons of England. He has held the posts of House Surgeon; Junior and Senior Resident Accoucheur at the London Hospital; and House Physician at the Royal Chest Hospital. He was for more than three years Resident Surgical Officer at the Poplar Hospital for Accidents, London. E.

The firm will in future be known as Drs Higgs and Goodwin —

Yours faithfully
Raymond. M. Higgs.

A 1907 letter from Dr Higgs of Toronto House, 384 High Street, the Carter's Green Medical Centre (see page 17). The letter reassures patients about a new partner. (Dr R. Rimmer)

Martin Dunne, glaziers and plumbers, situated at Dartmouth Square. An extensive range of bathroom fittings is on display in the unusual first-floor showroom. (A.H. Price)

Austin 7 vans outside Electromobile, Carter's Green, 1937. The firm, which specialised in auto electrics and fuel injection, was started in the 1920s by Lewis Nurse and sold in 1965 because of his ill health. The site is now occupied by Shaftesbury House, an office block housing the *Express & Star* and the Sandwell Education Department. (D. Nurse)

Webb & Son, undertakers, Hill Top. (A.H. Price)

West Bromwich Building Society staff, 20 April 1940. Back row, left to right: Miss Taylor, Carter, McDonald, Greatbatch, Johnson, Cookson, Brown, Stobart, Barton, Price, Bitin, Miss Breaze. Middle row: Miss Eaton, Carpenter, Swinnington, Mr Lloyd Williams (Assistant Secretary), Mr J. Scott Wright (Manager), Stephens, Baker, Scoby, Storton, Miss Jones. Front row: Irwin, Richards and Phipps. Absentee: Siddons (on military service). (West Bromwich Building Society)

TWENTIETH ANNUAL REPORT

OF THE

West Bromwich Permanent Building Society.

FELLOW SHAREHOLDERS,

Twenty years have elapsed since the formation of the West Bromwich Permanent Building Society: the close of the twentieth financial year brings with it to your Committee the duty of submitting to your perusal and consideration the accompanying Balance Sheet and Statement of Accounts. By a comparison with former accounts it will be seen that the Receipts exceed those of any previous year.

During the past year there have been paid 10 completed Investing Shares amounting to £1,200, and there has been written off during the year £4,974 7s. 6d. upon completed Mortgage Shares. The advances upon Property for the same period amount to £11,856 18s. 4d. All the securities have been carefully considered by your Committee, and they are held to be sufficient and ample · At the present time the society consists of 1005 Members, who hold altogether 1696¼ Shares, which represents a capital being subscribed for, of £203,550. Last year the numbers were respectively 933 and 1662¼, which shows a nett increase of 72 Members and 34 Shares, although the past year has been one of Mercantile depression, which has continued for an unprecedented length of time.

The nett Profit amounts to £4115 8s. 4d. which will yield a dividend of 7¾ per cent., and the Profit will be apportioned at the rate of 1s. 6½d. in the Pound. This satisfactory state of affairs has been attained without having recourse to any forcing process, and your Committee believe the whole of the large business of this Society is healthy and natural.

During the first half of the financial year ending April, applications for advances came in slowly, and large balances were lying comparatively unproductive in the hands of your Bankers. Under these circumstances your committee were of opinion that the time had arrived to pay off all the old Depositors who had been receiving 5 per cent. Interest, unless they were willing for their deposits to remain at 4 per cent, being the uniform rate paid upon all recent deposits. This alteration has been accomplished.

The Old Offices being too small to meet the requirements of a large and still growing business, your Committee decided to take upon a Lease more commodious Premises, and build New Offices at a cost of £181 6s. 1d. Towards this outlay the Lessors agreed to allow £42, leaving a balance of £139 6s. 1d. to be provided by the Society. In part payment or reduction of this balance, there has been written off this year £11 6s. 1d., and the remainder it is proposed to write off by 13 Annual Instalments of £10 each, thus spreading the payment for new offices over a term of 14 years.

This Society has now reached such a magnitude that a large new business each year is requisite to keep it increasing, as it has done in previous years; but the extended constituency now composing the Society renders it easy to maintain it in its present proud position, if each Member will take an interest in extending the Society's operations.

Signed on behalf of the Committee,

REUBEN FARLEY,

President.

May 31st, 1869.

The West Bromwich Building Society was founded on 23 April 1849 by twenty men of the town and district. They were: Edwin Bretell, George Coleman, Charles Cottrell, William Dangerfield, Solomon Evans, George Hall, John Harley, Joseph Hughes, Richard Jesson, W.H. Lewis, Henry Millward, John Sedgley, Lot Shakespeare, James P. Sharp, Edwin Silvester, Enoch Silvester, James Steventon, Robert Squires, William Upton and Samuel Withers. They met in the Wesleyan School Rooms which used to stand in Paradise Street, a site later occupied by the St George's cinema. The first 'regular' office was opened at 402 Lower High Street in 1854. Between 1863 and 1873 the society grew with members increasing from 451 to 1,588 and assets rising from £42,124 to £104,407. This annual report dates from this period and refers to the new offices at 298 High Street.

Frederick William Stamps, President of West
Bromwich Building Society and Chairman of
the Board of Directors, 1946. In 1949 – the year
of the Society's centenary – it had assets of
£5,059,245. (West Bromwich Building Society)

John D. Baker JP, FCA, FRSA of Walsall
became Chairman in 1992 at a time when the
Society lay twenty-second in the rankings of
building societies, with assets of £1 billion
compared with £479 in 1851. In 1999 the
society celebrates its 150th year of existence.

CHAPTER SIX

LEISURE

*An aerial view of West Bromwich Albion's new stadium, November 1997.
(D. Wilkins, First House Photography)*

West Bromwich Albion, winners of the FA Cup, 1888. Back row, left to right: W. Aldridge, E. Horton, H. Green, G. Timmins, R. Roberts, C. Perry, J. Wilson. Front row: G. Woodhall, W.I. Bassett, J.M. Bayliss (captain), T. Pearson. (B. Wilkes)

West Bromwich Albion, 1891/2. Albion's cup-winning team is seen here with the trophy. Left to right: Bassett, Nicholson, Reynolds, McLeod, Reader, Nicholls, Perry, Pearson, Groves, McCulloch, Geddes. This was the last FA Cup Final to have been played at the Kennington Oval. Albion beat rivals Aston Villa 3–0. (B. Wilkes)

England versus Ireland, 1902. This photo was taken in Ireland and Albert Wilkes senior, who was a half-back, is on the extreme left in the back row. (B. Wilkes)

West Bromwich Albion, 1910 second division champions. Back row, left to right: W. Barber (Trainer), J. Manners, D.G. Nurse (Director), R. Betteley, H. Pearson, W.I. Bassett (Chairman), R. Pailor, S. Bowser, H. Wright, G. Baddeley, F. Everiss (Secretary). Middle row: H. Keys (Director), R. McNeal, F. Buck, J. Pennington, J. Smith, Maj H. Ely (Director). Front row: F. Waterhouse, W. Wollaston, A. Lloyd. (BCS/BCM)

West Bromwich Albion, 1913/14. Back row, left to right: S. Richardson, Riddle, Crutchley, Shore, Pearson, Wright, Moorwood, Waterfall, Paddock (Assistant Trainer). Second row: W. Barber (Trainer), Reed, Deacey, Morris, Poulton, Lewis, Steer, Jackson, Wood, Buck, Baddeley, Harrison (Groundsman). Seated: McNeal, Cook, Waterhouse, Bentley, Pennington, Smith, Gregory, Shearman. Front: Jephcott, Hackett, Swift, Lloyd, Mann, Donald, Newell. (BCS/BCM)

West Bromwich Albion, FA Cup winners, 1930/31. Back row, left to right: F. Everiss (Secretary), J. Everiss (Director), L.J. Nurse (Director), H.F. Pearson, W.I. Bassett (Chairman), E. Smith (Assistant Secretary), J.S. Round JP (Director), Maj H. Wilson Keys (Director), F.W.M. Reed (Trainer). Middle row: W. Richardson, J. Edwards, T.W. Gidden (Captain), T.P. Magee, J.H. Carter, S. Wood. Front: J. Cookson, H.F. Trentham, W. Richardson, E. Sandford, G.E. Shaw, A.R. Finch. (B. Wilkes)

West Bromwich Albion, winners of the FA Cup, 1931. Some of the triumphant players are seen here immediately after receiving the cup and winners' medals. Left to right: Carter, Richardson, Edwards, Glidden (Captain), Magee, Shaw, Sandford. (T. Matthews)

West Bromwich Albion, FA Cup Final squad, 1935. Back row, left to right: F. Reed (trainer), Maj H. Wilson Keys, Trentham, Pearson, Carter, Mr J.S. Round JP (Director), Mr C. Jephcott (Director). Middle row: Mr L.J. Nurse (Director), W. Richardson, W.G. Richardson, Mr W.L. Bassett JP (Chairman), Glidden (Captain), Sandford, Mr F. Everiss (Secretary) Front: Gale, Edwards, Shaw, Murphy, Boyes, Sankey. (T. Matthews)

A programme from the 1935 Cup Final between West Bromwich Albion and Sheffield Wednesday. (A.S. Andrews)

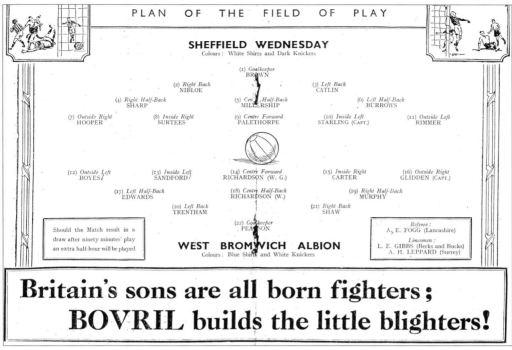

PLAN OF THE FIELD OF PLAY

SHEFFIELD WEDNESDAY
Colours : White Shirts and Dark Knickers

(1) *Goalkeeper*
BROWN

(2) *Right Back*   (3) *Left Back*
NIBLOE   CATLIN

(4) *Right Half-Back*   (5) *Centre Half-Back*   (6) *Left Half-Back*
SHARP   MILLERSHIP   BURROWS

(7) *Outside Right*   (8) *Inside Right*   (9) *Centre Forward*   (10) *Inside Left*   (11) *Outside Left*
HOOPER   SURTEES   PALETHORPE   STARLING (Capt.)   RIMMER

(12) *Outside Left*   (13) *Inside Left*   (14) *Centre Forward*   (15) *Inside Right*   (16) *Outside Right*
BOYES   SANDFORD   RICHARDSON (W. G.)   CARTER   GLIDDEN (Capt.)

(17) *Left Half-Back*   (18) *Centre Half-Back*   (19) *Right Half-Back*
EDWARDS   RICHARDSON (W.)   MURPHY

(20) *Left Back*   (21) *Right Back*
TRENTHAM   SHAW

(22) *Goalkeeper*
PEARSON

Should the Match result in a draw after ninety minutes' play an extra half-hour will be played

WEST BROMWICH ALBION
Colours : Blue Shirts and White Knickers

Referee :
A. E. FOGG (Lancashire)
Linesmen :
L. E. GIBBS (Berks and Bucks)
A. H. LEPPARD (Surrey)

Britain's sons are all born fighters;
BOVRIL builds the little blighters!

A diagram showing how the teams lined up for the 1935 Cup Final together with an appropriate advertisement! (A.S. Andrews)

West Bromwich Albion, 1954 FA Cup winners. Back row, left to right: J Kennedy, S. Williams, J. Dudley, J. Sanders, A. Fitton (Trainer), R. Barlow, J. Dugdale, L. Millard. Front row: F. Griffin, R. Ryan, R. Allen, J. Nicholls, G. Lee. (T. Matthews)

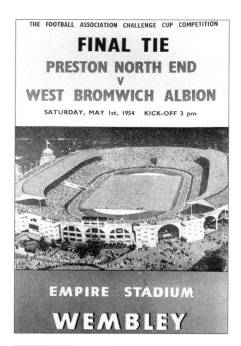

The cover of the historic programme which is now a
treasured souvenir of Albion's fantastic victory over
Preston North End in 1954. West Bromwich won 3–2
thanks to a late goal by Frank Griffin. (T. Matthews)

West Bromwich Albion, League Cup Winners, 1966. Back row, left to right: G. Lovett, S. Jones, R. Hope,
J. Astle, D. Fraser. Middle row: G. Williams, G. Howshall, R. Fairfax, R. Potter, D. Campbell, R. Cram.
Front row: J. Hagan (Manager), T. Brown, I. Collard, J. Kaye, C. Clark, A. McPherson (Trainer). (T. Matthews)

West Bromwich Albion after their 1-0 FA Cup win over Everton in 1968. Standing, left to right: D. Fraser, D. Clarke, J. Osborne, T. Brown, G. Lovett, J. Astle, J. Talbut. Crouching: I. Collard, G. Williams, C. Clark and R. Hope. (T. Matthews)

Dan Nurse came from Wolverhampton Wanderers as right half and was immediately made West Bromwich Albion's captain in 1900. A strong and determined player, his value lay in his ability to get the best out of the team on the field. He later became a director. (D. Nurse)

Dartmouth Park, 1909. The Earl of Dartmouth had leased 56 acres to the Council in 1877 as a park. (Dr C. Hollingsworth)

Carpet bedding, Dartmouth Park, 1913. Floral displays such as this became a tradition which was maintained by gardeners such as Reg Phillips (see page 121). (Dr C. Hollingsworth)

The Farley Fountain in Dartmouth Park, 1912.
It had been erected the previous year. (Dr C.
Hollingsworth)

Farley Fountain in the High Street, 1998.
This had originally been erected at Dartmouth
Square in memory of Elizabeth Farley by her
son, Alderman Farley, in 1885, but was
removed to Dartmouth Park in 1911 while
underground toilets were built on the site. In
the late 1960s the fountain was moved within
the park to make way for road improvements.
After a campaign by the Civic Pride Society it
was resited in the High Street in the 1970s.

War Memorial, Dartmouth Park. This card was posted on 3 August 1927. (A.H. Price)

The Bowling Green, Farley Park, 1925. This park was given to the town by Alderman Farley in 1890; it was situated in an area where he had lived and for which he had particular affection. (BCS/BCM)

George VI's coronation parade, 1937. This photograph was taken by Mr L. Nurse. (D. Nurse)

Territorial Army camp, 1915. (BCS/BCM)

West Bromwich teachers' Helyg Mountaineering Week, February 1958. Left to right: Reg Mallett, Ray Highfield, Bert Wright, Ian Tucker, H. Young, D. Grevel, Chas Chester, Pat Tivadale, Glyn Hughes, Ray Underhill, Harold White, B. Keift, Ted Hutton, Pete Henk, Geoff Robinson, Brian Wilkes. (B. Wilkes)

The picnic: Albert Wilkes (the baby) with his mother and aunt (little girl), 1904. The teapot reflects the photographer and proud father, Albert Wilkes senior. (B. Wilkes)

CHAPTER SEVEN

HOUSES

The sixteenth- and seventeenth-century Oak House was bought by Reuben Farley, who renovated it and gave it to the town in 1898 as a museum along with 4 acres of land. (Dr C. Hollingsworth)

West Bromwich Manor House before restoration, 1957. West Bromwich Corporation had bought the derelict property in 1950 to demolish it. From the 1880s it had been tenements. After a campaign from conservationists and architects, such as James A. Stafford and Frederick Charles, restoration was begun. (Dr J. Lester)

The Manor House undergoing restoration, October 1958. (Dr J. Lester)

The Manor House, December 1957. (Dr J. Lester)

The Manor House gatehouse, 1959. It is thought that this part of the house may date from the early seventeenth century; it bears some similarity to the gatehouse at Stokesay Castle in Shropshire. (Dr J. Lester)

The Manor House gatehouse, 1959. (Dr J. Lester)

The Manor House gatehouse, October 1959. (Dr J. Lester)

The Manor House hall, 1959. This part of the house has been dated to about 1275. Ansells adapted it to licensed premises in 1960. (Dr J. Lester)

Bishop Francis Asbury (Keith Cheetham) and a Black Countryman (Tony Dunn), outside the Bishop Asbury Cottage at Great Barr. This picture was taken prior to their departure in March 1992 for the American Airlines Travel Show in Dallas. (J.K. Cheetham)

Sandwell Hall, 1911. Originally the seat of the Whorwood family (see page 35), it was built on the site of the Priory. The Dartmouth family acquired it in 1701 and rebuilt it to the design of Francis Smith of Warwick. The Earl had moved to Patshull by 1853 and the Hall was used by various institutions including a poor children's school, a ladies' school, a home for distressed gentlewomen, a mental asylum and a home for mental defectives until its demolition in 1926. The Sandwell Park Lodge now stands on the roundabout at Junction 1 of the M5. The last child to be born in Sandwell Valley was Doreen Tinsley (née Phillips), whose father was a gardener (see page 121). (Dr C. Hollingsworth)

Charlemont Hall was built in about 1656 by the Lowe family of Lyndon, and was originally known as Crump Hall. In 1913 Thomas Jesson bought it, then Col. Bagnall of Bagnall's Ironworks. The last owner was Mrs Thomas Jones, wife of a former Town Clerk of Wednesbury. It was demolished just after the First World War. Charlemont was laid out as a 'garden city' in the 1920s. (BCS/BCM)

The home of John Johnson Shaw (see page 27). (BCS/BCM)

Mr. J. J. SHAW, M.Sc., C.B.E.

J.J. Shaw (1873–1948), with John Milne, perfected a seismograph in 1913. Shaw with his assistant C.F.C. Spencer ran a production line in Shaw's greenhouse, exporting the seismograph for around £100. Shaw became eminent in the seismological community and well known to the public as he popularised the science. In 1946 he retired and Hilger and Watts took over the production. One of his instruments was given by his son, H.V. Shaw, to the Lapworth Museum, University of Birmingham. The portrait was drawn by Arthur Arrowsmith. (*Express & Star*)

Highfield House, *c.* 1920. The house originated as four individual dwellings built between 1804 and 1839. The Council acquired it in 1922 and only the intervention of the Second World War prevented it being demolished to make way for a major civic buildings scheme. After the war the Garden of Remembrance was laid out and officially opened in 1951 by Admiral Sir John Cunningham. (BCS/BCM)

Highfield House is now the Register Office.

CHAPTER EIGHT

PEOPLE

Alderman Reuben Farley JP, who was five times mayor and a great benefactor of the town, is commemorated on the clock tower at Carter's Green. Another panel shows Oak House which he presented to the town as a museum (see page 111).

Kenrick & Jefferson Board, 1953. Left to right: A. Wynn Kenrick, E. Peter Kenrick, Edward Jefferson (Chairman), T. Kenneth Jefferson, T. Jefferson Cottrell. Kenrick & Jefferson were described as 'Printers to the World'. (K&J)

John Archibald Kenrick JP was elected to the Borough Council in 1906 and became mayor in 1911. Although Joint Managing Director of Archibald Kenrick & Sons, he also served as Chairman of Kenrick & Jefferson between 1920 and 1933. He was made a Freeman of the Borough just before his death in 1933. (K&J)

Photographer Albert Wilkes hard at work on the task of restoring or replacing sixty-four photographs of FA Cup winners since 1872, which were lost or damaged in a fire in 1967 in the shareholders' room at The Hawthorns. (B. Wilkes)

Mr Reg Phillips, a former West Bromwich parkkeeper, dedicated most of his working life to keeping the town in bloom at Dartmouth Park and Hill Top Park until his retirement in 1966. He died in 1996 aged ninety and a bench has been dedicated to his memory at Hill Top Park. (Mrs D. Tinsley)

Betty Boothroyd MP with Principal Nick Brown of the Sandwell Technical College. He retired in 1982 prior to the amalgamation of the Warley and West Bromwich colleges to form Sandwell College of Further Education (SCOFE). (J.S. Hunt)

Betty Boothroyd MP with Stan Hill, Chairman of the Black Country Society and Editor of *The Blackcountryman*. When Betty Boothroyd first took her seat as an MP for West Bromwich on 12 May 1973, she was accompanied by the last Mayor of West Bromwich, Alderman S.E.T. Martin and his wife. Local government reorganisation in 1974 brought about the creation of Sandwell Metropolitan Borough Council.

Rt Hon Betty Boothroyd MP, Speaker of the House of Commons, with Alan Pitt JP, B.Soc.Sci., Chairman of West Bromwich Magistrates, at a Training Day for JPs at the West Bromwich Moat House Hotel, 1996. (P.J. Elliott)

Lord Brookes of West Bromwich outside Garrington's Forge, Bromsgrove, which he established as one of the largest forges in the world, 1967. At the time he was Chairman and Managing Director of Garrington's. (Lord Brookes/J.L. Edwards)

Lord Brookes presenting the Student of the Year award to Tony Rangeley at West Bromwich Town Hall, 30 October 1979. The prize had been donated by BRD, part of GKN. There was nothing unusual in an apprentice winning the BRD award, but Lord Brookes, a leading industrialist, had also been an apprentice in West Bromwich. Born Raymond P. Brookes, he attended the Lodge Estate Elementary School. At fourteen he left school owing to financial difficulties following the death of his father in 1918. He studied mechanical engineering, accountancy and commercial law part-time at Kenrick Technical College and by correspondence course. He was fortunate to serve an apprenticeship with Charles Bunn Ltd, Drop Forgers, Founders, Engineers and Metal Finishers, and rose to Managing Director by 1939. In 1941 he moved to Garrington's as Director and General Manager to spearhead munitions, especially naval shells. As Managing Director of Garrington's from 1951, he established BRD Aldridge, to finish castings made by Garrington's for jet engine turbo blades prior to the Korean War. He became Chairman of GKN from 1974 to 1982 and is currently Life President. (J.S. Hunt/ J.L. Edwards)

The actress Julie Walters went to Holly Lodge Grammar School, Smethwick, and Manchester Polytechnic, where she qualified as a teacher. She became famous for her part in *Educating Rita* and received the Variety Club of Great Britain's Award for Best Film Actress and the BAFTA award for Best Actress in 1983. She has achieved considerable success since that time, on stage, screen and television. (S. Hill/Miss J. Walters)

Brian Walden, the television presenter, journalist and former MP for Birmingham All Saints and for Ladywood was born in the Stone Cross area in 1932. He attended West Bromwich Grammar School, Queen's College and Nuffield College, Oxford, and was President of the Oxford Union in 1957. For his work as a television presenter (*Weekend World*, *The Walden Interview*, and *Walden*) he has been recognised with many prizes including the BAFTA Richard Dimbleby Award, *TV Times* Favourite TV Current Affairs Personality and the TV and Radio Industries Club ITV Personality of the Year. He published *The Walden Interviews* in 1990. (A.B. Walden)

ACKNOWLEDGEMENTS

This book is compiled from over 200 pictures borrowed from private owners. I am very indebted to them for their kindness and hope that I have not inadvertently omitted anyone's name.

Every effort has been made to contact owners of copyright photographs, where copyright did not rest with those who owned the prints.

Mrs F. Allen; Mrs M. Allen; Dr G. Allman; A.S. Andrews; John D. Baker; Mr & the late Mrs Bloor; I. Bott; J. Boulton; G. Brinsdon; Lord R. Brookes; Mrs E. Cartwright; J.K. Cheetham; M. Chesney; Pat Eden; J.L. Edwards; P.J. Elliott; *Express & Star*; the late W.K.V. Gale; F.C. & Mrs D. Hammond; Mrs M. Hemming; T. & Mrs J. Highfield; Stan Hill; K. Hodgkins; G. Hollick; Dr C. Hollingsworth; Revd Dr G. Hume; J.S. Hunt; H. Jefferson; Dr J. Lester; T. Matthews; R.J. Meller; N. Moore; N. Morris; Prof. O. Naddermier; S. & Mrs J. Nock; D. Nurse; P. O'Brien; G.R. Phillips; A.H. Price; G. Quinn; K. Reed; Dr R. Rimmer; Mrs A. Second; R.C. Shayler; K. Smith; Miss Pat Thomas; A.S. & Mrs D. Tinsley; Miss L. Tromans; P.F. Twine; A.B. Walden; I. Walden; Miss Ruth Waller; Miss J. Walters; J.S. Webb; M.F. White; B. & Mrs M. Wilkes; D. Wilkins; Ned Williams; W. Woodhouse; T. Workman.

Paul Hemming and Gareth Porter with the FA Cup at a benefit match at Dartmouth Cricket Club, 1968.

BRITAIN IN OLD PHOTOGRAPHS

SUTTON'S PHOTOGRAPHIC HISTORY OF TRANSPORT

To order any of these titles please telephone our distributor, Littlehampton Book Services on 01903 828800
For a catalogue of these and our other titles please ring Emma Leitch on 01453 731114